Telepathic Wanderers Vol. 1
Written by Yasutaka Tsutsui
Illustrated by Sayaka Yamazaki

Translation -	Asuka Yoshizu
English Adaptation -	Stormcrow Hayes
Copy Editors -	Hope Donovan and Eric Althoff
Retouch and Lettering -	Bowen Park
Production Artist -	Jason Milligan
Cover Design -	Kyle Plummer
Editor -	Troy Lewter
Digital Imaging Manager -	Chris Buford
Production Managers -	Jennifer Miller and Mutsumi Miyazaki
Managing Editor -	Lindsey Johnston
VP of Production -	Ron Klamert
Publisher and E.I.C. -	Mike Kiley
President and C.O.O. -	John Parker
C.E.O. -	Stuart Levy

A  Manga

TOKYOPOP Inc.
5900 Wilshire Blvd. Suite 2000
Los Angeles, CA 90036

E-mail: info@TOKYOPOP.com
Come visit us online at www.TOKYOPOP.com

ISBN: 1-59532-938-2

First TOKYOPOP printing: November 2005

10 9 8 7 6 5 4 3 2 1

Printed in the USA

Volume 1

Story By
Yasutaka Tsutsui

Art By
Sayaka Yamazaki

HAMBURG // LONDON // LOS ANGELES // TOKYO

Contents

とっ
とっ
とっ

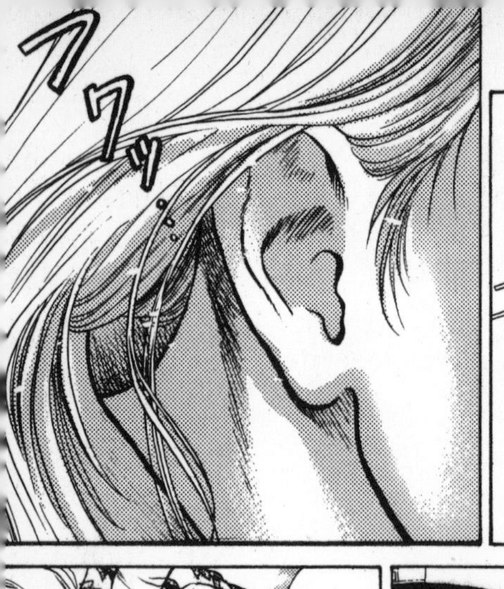
フワッ

ニャー

……
Kanpyou
3040
1kgX14
seven

1kgX14
seven

AFTER ALL THIS TIME, I'M FINALLY HOME.
カッ
カッ
カッ

キ
キッ
I WONDER...
...IF I COULD MOVE BACK HERE?
AH!
HEY...! WATCH WHERE YOU'RE GOING!
フゥッ..
......
SHE DIDN'T HAVE TO GET SO ANGRY...
HMPH!
ブツ
ブツ
PEDES-TRIANS NEVER LOOK WHERE THEY'RE WALKING!

Episode 0: Homecoming--Part 1

NANASE HIDA?

Sold Here

Cigars

YEP. IT WAS HER.

HAVEN'T SEEN HER SINCE JUNIOR HIGH.

Seaweed

OH...

I HEARD SHE SKIPPED HIGH SCHOOL TO WORK IN TOKYO.

SO WHAT'S SHE DOING BACK IN TOWN?

IS SHE STILL PRETTY?

HELL YEAH...! SHE'S GORGEOUS! AND SHE HAS ONE FINE A--

HI. DO YOU CARRY FLOWERS AND CIGA-RETTES?

HEY!
IT'S HIDA!
!

HOW LONG HAS IT BEEN?
FIVE YEARS?
THAT'S RIGHT! ***FIVE YEARS!*** DO YOU REMEMBER US?

Y- YOU'RE ***YATA-KUN*** AND ***KAWA-NO-KUN***... AREN'T YOU?

......

......
UM...
HUH?
HOW LONG ARE YOU IN TOWN?
PLEASE-- HAVE A SEAT...!
WANT SOME TEA?
I NEED TO PICK UP SOME FLOWERS...

SHE'S SOO BEAUTIFUL...! DO YOU THINK SHE'S AN ACTRESS?
DOES IT MATTER?! JUST LOOK AT THAT NICE, ROUND ...

THROB
....

Souvenirs & Coffee

HIDA!

I *THOUGHT* IT WAS *YOU!*

FUJITA-SENSEI...

IT'S BEEN A LONG TIME.

YOU'VE BLOSSOMED INTO QUITE A BEAUTY. I ALMOST DIDN'T RECOGNIZE YOU.

ARE YOU LIVING IN TOKYO?

OH! WANNA GRAB SOME LUNCH?

I'M SORRY... BUT I HAVE TO FINISH RUNNING ERRANDS.
O-OH.
I-I SEE. OKAY, THEN...

Tombstone: Hida Family

I'M SORRY I'VE NEGLECTED YOU FOR SO LONG...

...BUT...

...I'M PLANNING ON MOVING BACK HERE FOR GOOD.

I WANT...

...TO LIVE A NORMAL LIFE LIKE EVERYONE ELSE...

Kawano Liqu Stor

WHERE IS SHE?

IS SHE REALLY COM-ING?

I TOLD YOU, SHE'LL BE HERE AFTER SHE TAKES CARE OF HER BUSINESS!!

DIDN'T YOU GET HER CELL PHONE NUMBER OR SOMETHING?!

Pour me another drink.

It's cold in here!

....

ARE YOU DONE WITH YOUR ERRANDS?

C'MON...

カチ
AHHH...
NOW THAT'S WHAT A CIGARETTE SHOULD TASTE LIKE!

MY DAD'S CIGA-RETTES!
バッ
HUH?!

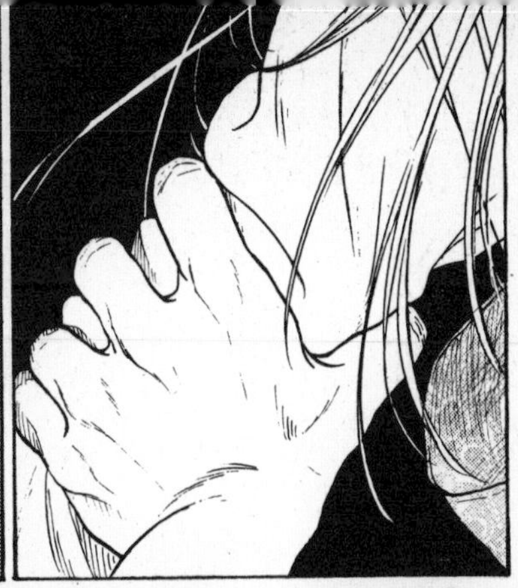

UNH ...!
H-HEY! L-LET GO...!

I'VE WAITED SUCH A LONG TIME TO SEE YOU...
...HIDA!

BY THE WAY, I THINK I SAW FUJITA-SENSEI EARLIER.

WHAT A MESS THAT WAS...
I'M GLAD HE WAS FIRED!
EWWW...! IS HE STILL IN TOWN?!
AFTER THE SCANDAL BROKE, THE MEDIA CONVERGED ON OUR SCHOOL.
THE FACT THAT TOKITA WAS, YOU KNOW, "NOT RIGHT IN THE HEAD," MADE IT WORSE.
NOT TO MENTION IT HAPPENED RIGHT BEFORE GRADUATION, WHICH SUCKED.
HIDA-SAN TESTIFIED, DIDN'T SHE?

SHE USED TO TAKE GOOD CARE OF TOKITA.

THAT'S RIGHT!

"TOKI-TA-KUN DIDN'T DO IT!"

"IT MUST HAVE BEEN TOKITA!"

"WHO DID THIS?!"

SHE WAS ALWAYS SO PRO-TECTIVE OF HIM.

I ONCE ASKED HER WHY SHE CARED FOR HIM...

...AND SHE SAID IT'S BECAUSE HE'S HONEST AND NEVER LIES.

HIDA WAS ALWAYS SWEET.

YOU USED TO BORROW MONEY FROM HER AND NEVER PAY HER BACK.

THAT'S BECAUSE SHE NEVER ASKED ME TO PAY HER BACK.

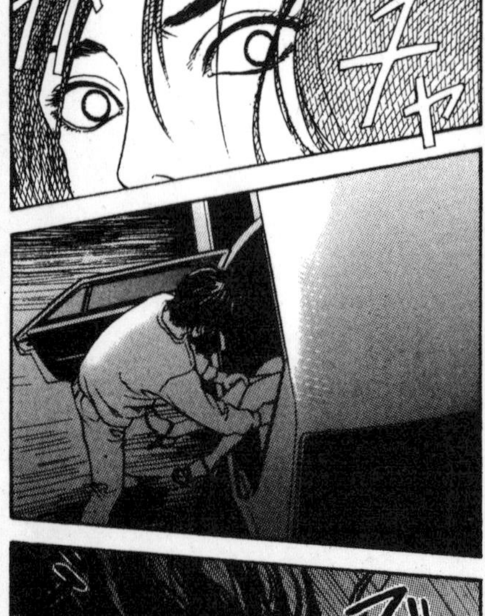
ガチャ

ズル…
……

くいっ

WELCOME TO MY ROOM.

SURE, THE APARTMENT'S A BIT DILAPIDATED ...
...BUT WHAT ELSE CAN YOU EXPECT FROM A CONDEMNED BUILDING?

I'M THIRTY-EIGHT YEARS OLD...

...I DON'T HAVE A GIRLFRIEND... AND THE ONLY JOB I CAN GET...
...IS BACK-BREAKING CRAP A MONKEY COULD DO!

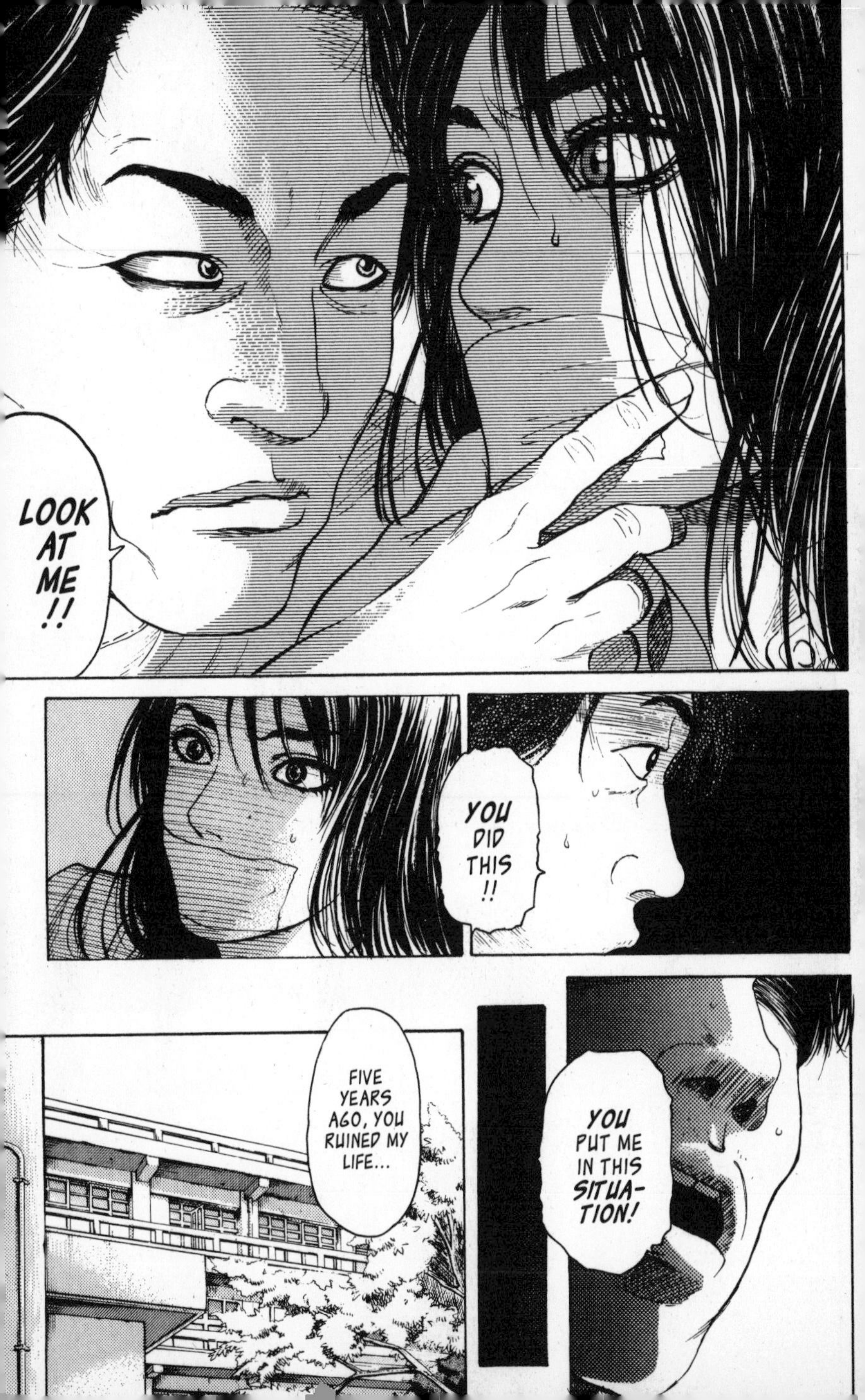

LOOK AT ME!!

YOU DID THIS!!

YOU PUT ME IN THIS SITUATION!

FIVE YEARS AGO, YOU RUINED MY LIFE...

HE WAS ALREADY DEAD...
...WHEN I FOUND HIM.

THE POLICE BELIEVED ME.
AND THEN **YOU** SHOWED UP...

"I SAW THIS TEACHER SHOVE TOKITA-KUN..."

ピッ
WHAT THE FUCK DID YOU SEE?!
TELL ME, BITCH!!
......
WHAT DID I DO?!
ビ
I WAS INNOCENT!
BUT DID ANYBODY LISTEN?! OH, NOOO!
SO YEAH... IT WAS PRETTY MUCH THE WORST EXPERIENCE OF MY ENTIRE FUCKING LIFE.

...MY WIFE... MY CAREER...
...I LOST EVERYTHING...
...POOF! ALL GONE!!
DURING THE LAST FIVE YEARS...
UMPH!
EXCEPT THIS WASN'T SOME CHARMING LITTLE MAGIC TRICK...
THIS WAS *YOU* RUINING MY LIFE WITH YOUR *FILTHY LIES!*

......

THAT YOUR PARENTS WERE KILLED IN A CAR ACCIDENT.

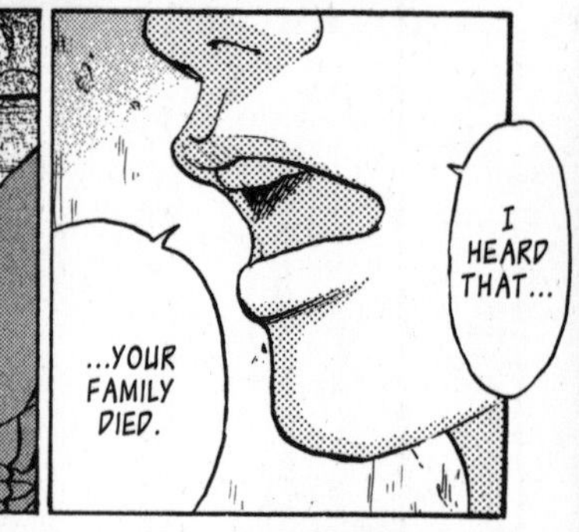
I HEARD THAT...
...YOUR FAMILY DIED.

GUESS THAT JUST MEANS NO ONE WILL MISS YOU...
...DOESN'T IT?

!
LET ME GO!!
UNH!
L- LET ME... G-GO ...
NO!!

NOT UNTIL I'VE HURT *YOU* AS MUCH AS YOU HURT *ME!!*
CASH
WHY DID YOU *DO IT?!* DID YOU THINK IT WAS *FUNNY?!*
N-NO...
WHAT?! WHAT WAS *THAT*, BITCH?!

SHE WAS AL-WAYS...
...LOOKING DOWN ON ME!

THINK-ING BACK...
...I EVEN HATED HER WHEN SHE WAS A KID...

I HATE THAT KIND OF ARROGANCE!!
I HATE PEOPLE WHO LOOK DOWN ON ME!!
THEY DON'T KNOW ME! THEY KNOW NOTHING ABOUT ME!!

....

"NANASE... YOU SHOULD NEVER TELL ANYONE ABOUT YOUR GIFT."

"OTHER PEOPLE DON'T HAVE YOUR ABILITES."

"CHILDREN CAN BE CRUEL WHEN THEY KNOW SOMEONE'S DIFFERENT FROM THEM."
"I JUST DON'T WANT YOU TO BE HURT."

"SO... WHATEVER YOU DO..."

"...NEVER FORGET ABOUT OUR TALK!"
DAD...

!!

AHHH!
IT BURRRNS!!
ハァ ハッ
SUFFER.
HEH... JUST A TASTE OF THINGS TO COME, WHORE.
FEEL MY PAIN.
ATONE FOR YOUR SINS!

ATONE FOR WHAT SINS?

WHAT...? DID I...?
WAS I TALKING UNDER MY BREATH...? HOW DID SHE--

YOU WEREN'T THINKING OUT LOUD.

WHAT?!
WHAT ?!
WHAT THE FUCK IS GOING ON?!
WHAT THE FUCK IS GOING ON?!
SHE'S... SHE'S READING MY MIND...!

トッ

THIS IS RIDICULOUS...! THIS IS...
SHE'S GUESSING SOMEHOW! YEAH! SHE'S JUST MAKING A LUCKY GUESS! THAT'S ALL...
SHE CAN'T...

SHE'S JUST TRYING TO FREAK ME OUT!
YEAH... THAT'S GOTTA BE IT!

I'M NOT TRYING TO FREAK YOU OUT.

IT'S NOT LUCK...

...AND IT'S NOT A GUESS.

W-WHA...

Episode 0: Homecoming--Part 1 END

Telepathic
Wanderers

ウッ..

Episode 0: Homecoming--Part 2

DO YOU WANT TO HEAR THE TRUTH?

I'LL TELL YOU...
...WHAT HAPPENED FIVE YEARS AGO.

I COULDN'T BELIEVE YOU DID IT. IT'S BAD ENOUGH THE KIDS TEASED HIM...
TOKITA WAS SLOW...SO HE NEEDED SPECIAL ATTENTION.
BUT INSTEAD, YOU ADDED TO HIS MISERY AND TORMENT.
......
SENSEI?
YES, HIDA?
I DON'T THINK WHAT YOU DID... WAS VERY APPROPRIATE.

I THINK YOU SHOULD...
...APOLOGIZE TO HIM.
W-WHAT ARE YOU TALKING ABOUT?
OH, DID I STEP ON SOME-THING?
I HARDLY NOTICED.
HEH... IT'S JUST A NOTE-BOOK...
...RIGHT, TOKITA?
......

NOW GET TO CLASS OR YOU'LL BE TARDY.
BECAUSE I WAS LATE...
...YOU MADE ME STAND FOR THE ENTIRE HOUR.

She was only a few seconds late to class.

Talk about harsh!

......

Whisper...

NO TALKING!!

TOKITA FOLLOWED YOU AFTER CLASS...

HE WANTED TO TALK TO YOU ABOUT MY PUNISHMENT.

WHY? HUH?
TELL ME WHY I SHOULD!
AND DON'T STUTTER! SPEAK CLEARLY!!
BAH! I DON'T HAVE TIME FOR THIS...!
FUH ...
FUH ...
FUJITA ...
DON'T *TOUCH* ME!

ISN'T THAT WHAT HAPPENED, TEACHER?
WEREN'T YOU...
...THE CAUSE OF HIS DEATH?
HOW ...?
HOW COULD SHE KNOW ?!

NOBODY WAS THERE!
......
NO...
I AM...
IT WASN'T MY FAULT...
...I AM ALWAYS...
...A GOOD PERSON!
THAT'S WHY I'M...
...PUNISHING THIS BITCH...
...FOR RUINING MY LIFE!!

I DIDN'T RUIN YOUR LIFE!
YOU CAN'T PUNISH ME FOR YOUR SINS.
YOU'RE JUST...
...AN EVIL MAN!
N-NO...
STOP!!
STOP IT!!
IT WAS YOUR FAULT!!

WHAT ...?!
WHAT KIND OF TRICK IS THIS?!
STOP TOYING WITH ME!!
PLEASE! STOP!!
IF SHE CAN READ MY MIND...
...THEN... THAT MEANS... AW, SHIT...
DON'T EVEN TRY TO MASK YOUR MIND. IT'S IMPOSSIBLE TO THINK ABOUT NOTHING.

OH...
...DEAR GOD...
HOW...?
HOW...?!
HOW CAN SHE TELL?
SHE'S A MONSTER !!
I'M NOT A MONSTER.
I THINK THE WORD YOU'RE LOOKING FOR IS...

...TELEPATH!!

TELEPATH?
IMPOSSIBLE! THERE'S NO SUCH THING AS--
--TELE-PATHY? WELL, I'M PROOF POSITIVE IT'S **REAL**, WOULDN'T YOU SAY?
HA... UH...
SHE GOT IT RIGHT... AGAIN!
AM I CRAZY?!
NO. YOU'RE NOT CRAZY.
OH...
...NO!!

......
HIS EMO- TIONS ...
...ARE FLOODING INTO MY HEAD!
PANIC, CONFU- SION, PAIN AND FEAR...
IF I'M NOT CAREFUL, WE COULD BOTH END UP...
...IN- SANE!
I HAVE NO CHOICE... I MUST STOP HIM!

IF I LET HIM LIVE...
...I'LL BE TREATED LIKE A MONSTER!
I'VE NO CHOICE... I HAVE TO OBLITERATE HIS MIND!

I'M SORRY!!
ガッ
YOU'RE RIGHT! EVERYTHING YOU'VE SAID IS ABSOLUTELY RIGHT!
I'VE DONE TERRIBLE THINGS IN MY LIFE BECAUSE I'VE BEEN SO FRUSTRATED!
I'M S-SORRY I HURT YOU...!
DON'T THINK!
KEEP TALKING!
S-SOMETHING IS WRONG WITH ME...
SPEAK BEFORE THINKING!!
FOCUS YOUR THOUGHTS!
I'M...
...I'M A FAILURE!

ぎゅうぅ…
AH...
FOR-GIVE...
WHY ARE YOU DOING THIS TO ME?!
AH!
I... I DON'T DESERVE THIS!
HOW **DARE** YOU **HUMILIATE** ME LIKE **THIS?!**
ARGH!
I'M THE ONLY ONE WHO'S BEEN **WRONGED!!**
HOW HAVE ***YOU*** BEEN WRONGED?!
YOU'RE ONLY GETTING WHAT YOU ***DESERVE!***
NO!!

PLEASE...
YOU MISUNDERSTOOD ME!
SOMEBODY HELP ME!
NOBODY CAN HELP YOU.
N-NO!!
GASP!
PLEASE...
PANT!
S-STOP...
GASP!
!

"TAKA-CHAN...
...COME HERE."
"TAKA-CHAN..."

"TAKA-CHAN... YOU ARE A **GREAT** CHILD."
"YOU'RE SO MUCH BETTER THAN THE OTHER KIDS."
"I'M SO PROUD OF YOU!"

DON'T LIE TO YOURSELF.
YOU'RE NOT GREAT.
YOU'RE NOTHING BUT A LYING MURDERER ...
...WHO'S GOING STRAIGHT TO HELL !!

I T-THINK I'M G-GONNA BE SICK...!

UGH... HURRAK!

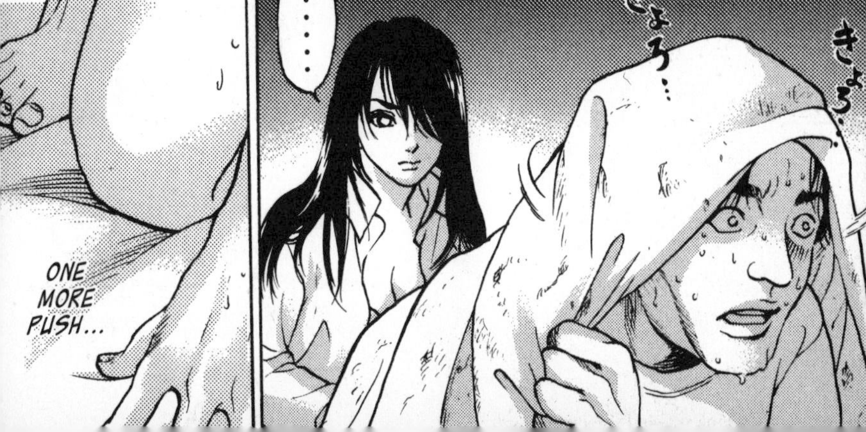

ゴク…
GRANDMA!
TELL HER, GRANDMA!
ズル…
ズル…
ズル…
HELP ME!
TELL HER I'M A GOOD KID!
WHERE ARE YOU?!
!

WAIT! I KNOW THAT DOOR !!
THIS ROOM...! IT'S...
... GRAND-MA'S !!

YOUR GRANDMOTHER'S DEAD.

HIS MIND... IT'S ABOUT TO SNAP!!

THERE! HIS MIND HAS SHAT-TERED!!
HIS MADNESS... IT'S DEVOURING ME!!

HUH?!

PANT
ザッ
ザッ
PANT
ザッ
PANT
PANT
PANT
GASP
PANT
PANT
PANT

DAD... THIS... IS...
コト..
...YOURS!

YOU'RE LEAVING? ALREADY ?!
I MEAN...
...WHERE WERE YOU LAST NIGHT?
SORRY ABOUT THAT. MY ERRANDS TOOK LONGER THAN I THOUGHT.
Yeah, well...
I GUESS IT CAN'T BE HELPED.
WE'LL JUST HAVE TO GET TOGETHER SOME OTHER TIME.
....

DAMN... I REALLY WANTED TO FUCK HER!

ONCE YOU CAN SEE INTO PEOPLE'S MINDS...

Episode 0: Homecoming–Part 2 END

Telepathic Wanderers

Telepathic Wanderers

Episode 1:
Two Psychics--Part 1

アアア
ザ
アアアア
ガタン
ゴン
ガタン
ガタン

ガタン
タン…
ガタン
since 1895
コーン
コーン
タタン

NYAAAAH!!

WAAAH!!

ハッ
タタン
タン

HUH ...

THANK GOD! IT WAS JUST A DREAM...!

?

BUT... IT FELT SO REAL...

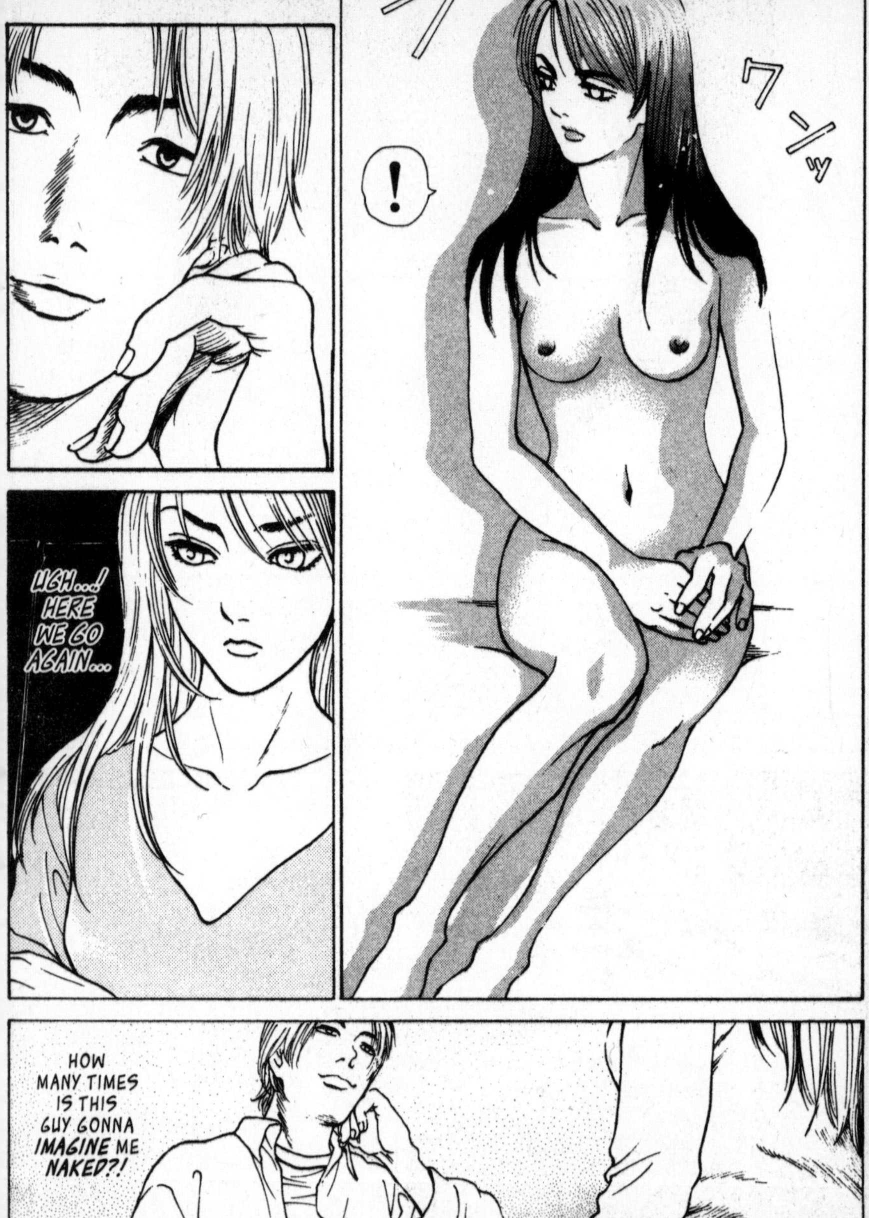
ワンッ
!
UGH...! HERE WE GO AGAIN...
HOW MANY TIMES IS THIS GUY GONNA *IMAGINE* ME *NAKED?!*

CUT IT OUT, YOU PERV!

HMM...

THIS RAIN HASN'T LET UP EVER SINCE I GOT ON THE TRAIN THIS EVENING...

NO! IT ISN'T POSSIBLE!

MAYBE...
...I SHOULD GET OFF AT THE NEXT STATION.
IT'S NOT LIKE I HAVE A SPECIFIC DESTINATION ANYWAY.

I JUST HOPE THERE ISN'T A LANDSLIDE...!
......
Oh!
MAYBE YOU DON'T KNOW THIS...
I DON'T THINK IT'S POSSIBLE.
...BUT LANDSLIDES OCCUR QUITE OFTEN IN THIS AREA!

ガタン・・
THERE! SEE THAT REDDISH SOIL?
IT'S VERY SOFT AND UNSTABLE!
タタン・・
DON'T YOU RE-MEMBER? THERE WAS ONE SEVERAL YEARS AGO...
"WHY DOESN'T SHE SHUT UP?!"
"WHAT AN IDIOT!"
"THOUGHT-LESS WOMAN... AND ON A NIGHT LIKE THIS..."
"IF WE DO CRASH, I HOPE SHE'S THE FIRST TO GO!"
"SHE'S SCARING MY CHILD!"

Sigh..
I GOTTA GET OUT OF HERE...! MAYBE I'LL GO TO THE BATH-ROOM...
I SHOULD PROBABLY FOLLOW HER...

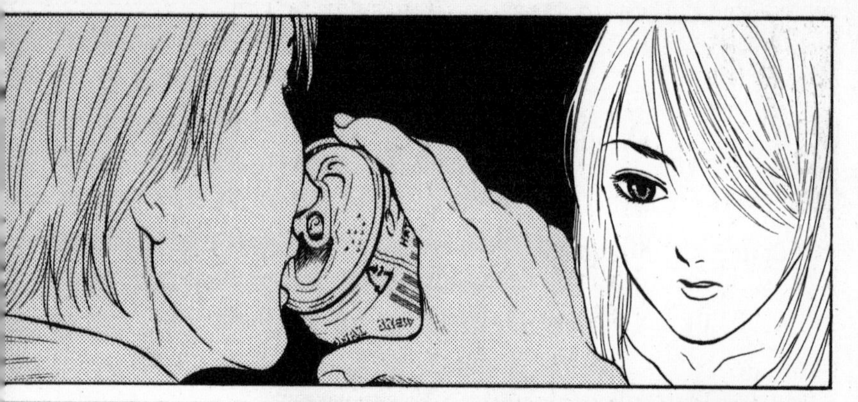

IF SHE'S GOING TO THE BATH-ROOM...

...I CAN TRAP HER LIKE THAT ONE CHICK THE OTHER DAY.

BESIDES... I HAVE A **KNIFE**...

...SO I'M SURE SHE WOULDN'T PUT UP A FIGHT!

TWO WOMEN AND A CHILD WERE BURIED BENEATH A ROCK...

I KNOW SHE'S JUST TALKING TO RELIEVE HER FEAR, BUT SHE'S SCARING THE OTHERS.

ERR... WHERE ARE YOU HEADED?

I SHOULD GET OFF WITH HER!

IT'S DANGEROUS TO WALK ALONE AT NIGHT.

NO KIDDING!

SHINODAGUCHI, EH...? MAYBE I SHOULD FOLLOW HER THERE...

THOSE LIPS!

THAT SOFT FLESH...

HER HARD, RUBY NIPPLES...

I WONDER IF SHE'S A PILLOW BITER...OR SQUEALER?

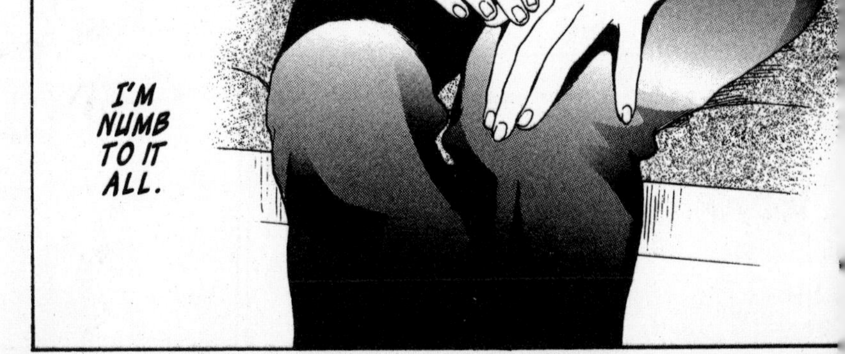

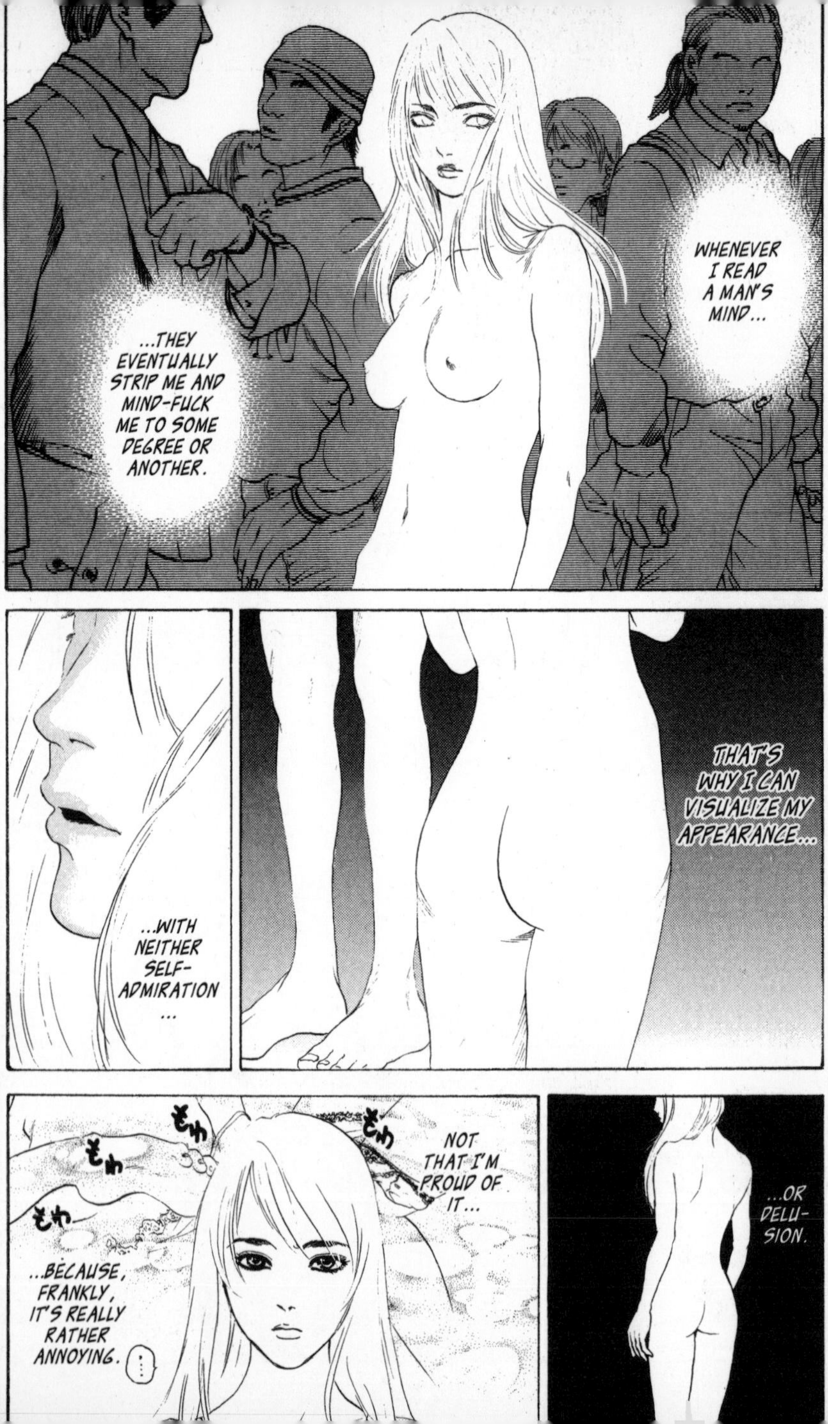

WHENEVER I READ A MAN'S MIND...

...THEY EVENTUALLY STRIP ME AND MIND-FUCK ME TO SOME DEGREE OR ANOTHER.

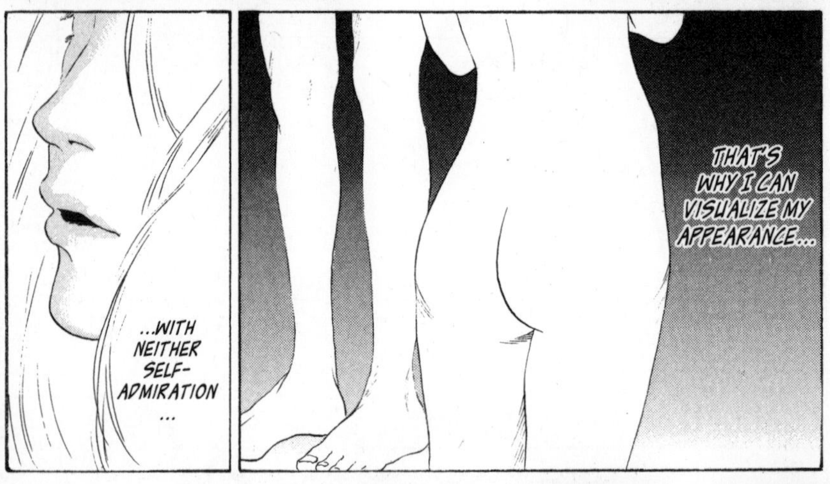

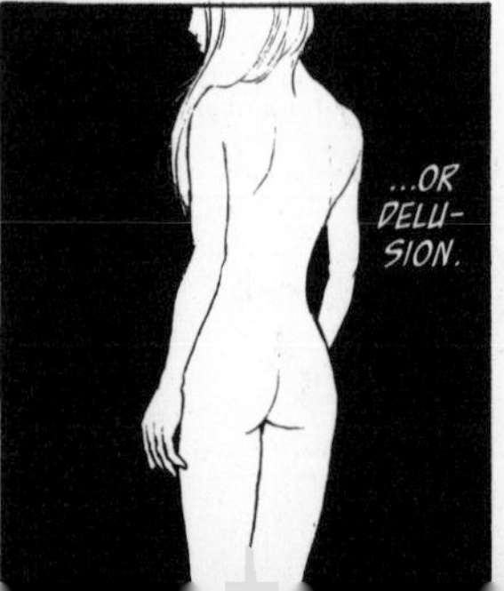

ニヤ
ニヤ…
HOWEVER... IF YOU ARE GOING TO PUT YOUR IMAGINATION INTO ACTION...

...THEN I'LL RESPOND ACCORDINGLY.

?
ガタン
ゴト
ガタン

WAAH! WAAH!
H-HUH...!
WAAAH!!
WAAAAH!!
うあ
WAAH!!
あ
WAAAH!!
ん

THAT CHILD...
HE'S DREAMING...
...THOUGH I CAN'T SEE IT CLEARLY.
WAAAH!
SEEMS LIKE IT'S ONE DOOZY OF A NIGHTMARE.
WAAAH!
WHERE'S HIS MOTHER?!
SHUT UP, ALREADY!
SHH!
WHAT NOW ...?!

YOU NEED TO BE QUIET! YOU'RE BOTHERING EVERYONE!
....

WHAT'S WRONG, HUH? WHATEVER IT IS, IT CAN'T BE THIS BAD!
JUST STOP CRYING, OKAY?!

OH...!

ROTTEN KID...!
YOU'RE GETTING A WHIPPING WHEN WE GET HOME!

!

WAAAH!!

SHHHH!!

NORIO!!

QUIET!!

......

WHAT...? DOES SHE HATE HER CHILD?!

!
NO... THERE'S SOMETHING MORE...

FEAR?!

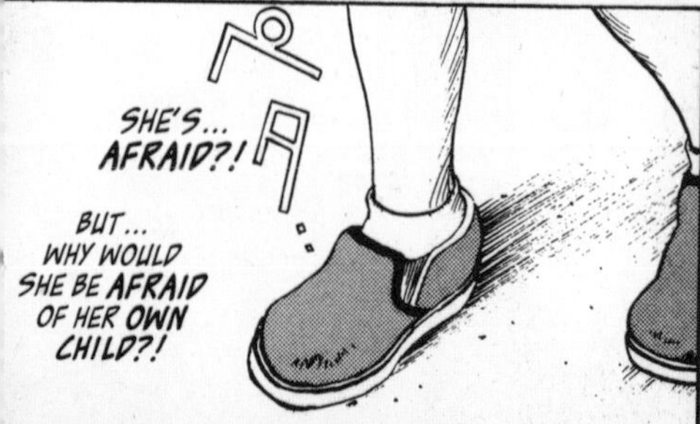
SHE'S... AFRAID?!
BUT... WHY WOULD SHE BE AFRAID OF HER OWN CHILD?!

W- WHAT?! WHAT NOW?!
I'M HUNGRY...

BUT HE'S SUCH A CUTE BOY...
YOU JUST ATE AN HOUR AGO!
YOU CAN WAIT 'TIL WE GET HOME!
......

BUT ...
GRRRRR
... MY BELLY ...

DAMN BRAT!
HE KNOWS I WON'T HIT HIM IN PUBLIC!

POOR BOY...
I WONDER IF I HAVE ANYTHING FOR HIM TO EAT?

カリーーーッ

WHOA!
YOU FEEL THAT BUMP?!

IT'S... IT'S PERFECTLY NORMAL...

I'M SURE...
...IT HAS NOTHING TO DO WITH MY DREAM...

ガタン
タタン…
BUT...I CAN'T GET IT OUT OF MY HEAD...!
ギク

THE DREAM!!
HE HAS THE SAME IMAGES IN HIS MIND AS IN MY DREAM!
IT'S SO VIVID... IT'S AS IF...
AS IF IT WERE... RECREATED!!
......
RE...
...CREATED?

WHAT?!
DID HE...
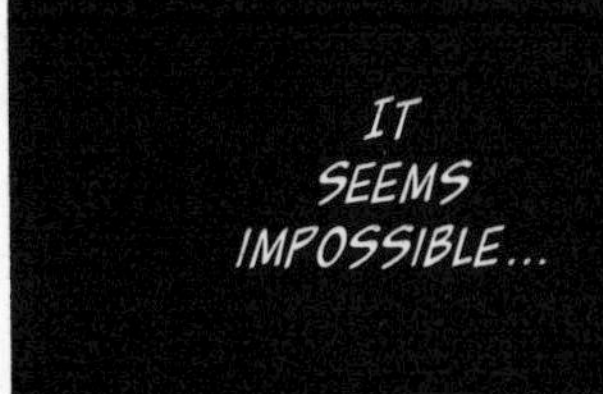
IT SEEMS IMPOSSIBLE...

...JUST READ MY MIND?!

COULD IT BE...? COULD SOMEONE ELSE HAVE MY POWERS?
I'VE ALWAYS WONDERED IF...MAYBE--
NO...! NO WAY!
IT CAN'T BE!! CAN IT...?

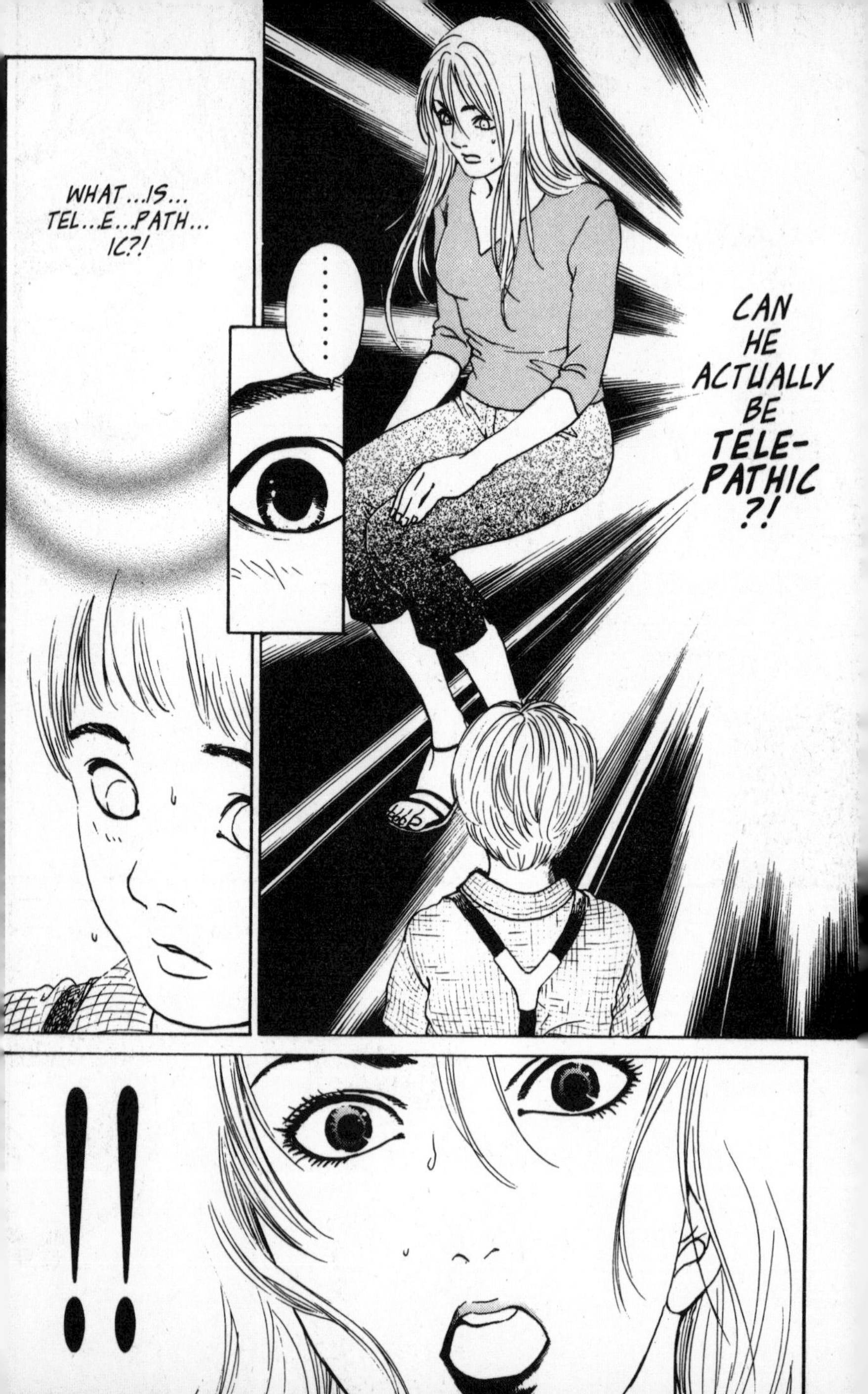
CAN HE ACTUALLY BE TELE-PATHIC?!
......
WHAT...IS... TEL...E...PATH... IC?!
!!

……
WHAT'S THIS? THE CREEPY BRAT'S SUDDENLY QUIET…
ビク
I… I CAN'T BELIEVE IT…
FOR THE FIRST TIME IN MY LIFE…
!

Episode 1: Two Psychics--Part 1 END

Episode 1: Two Psychics--Part 2

ガタン。
UNBELIEVABLE!!
ガタ

I WANT TO GET OFF THE TRAIN!
W- WHAT?
M- MOMMY?

IT'S GONNA CRASH!

OH...!

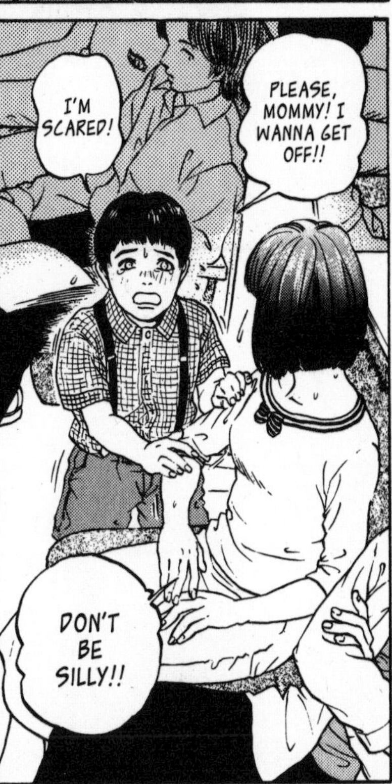
PLEASE, MOMMY! I WANNA GET OFF!!
I'M SCARED!
DON'T BE SILLY!!

SHIT... HE THINKS MY DREAM IS A PREMONITION...

NORIO!!
LET'S GO! NOW!!
WE HAVE TO!!

NOOO!! I DON'T WANNA DIE!!
……

IT'S OKAY, NORIO.
?
WE'RE NOT GOING TO GET INTO AN ACCIDENT.
WE'LL BE OKAY.
ビクッ

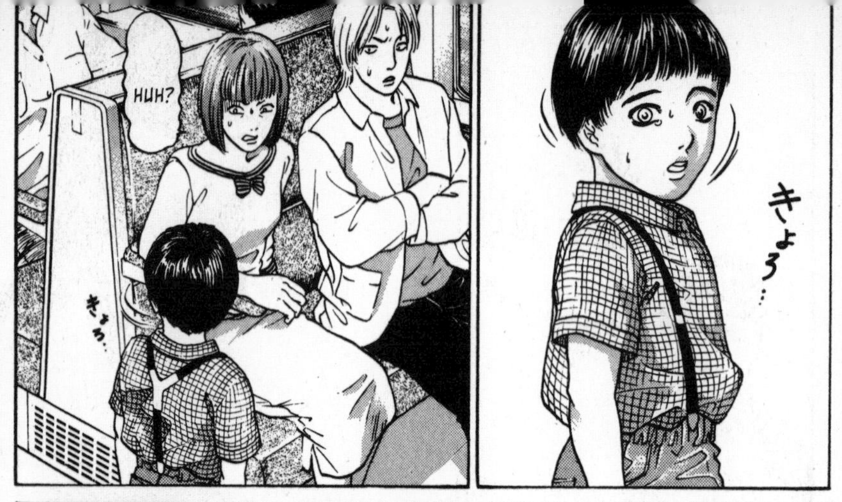

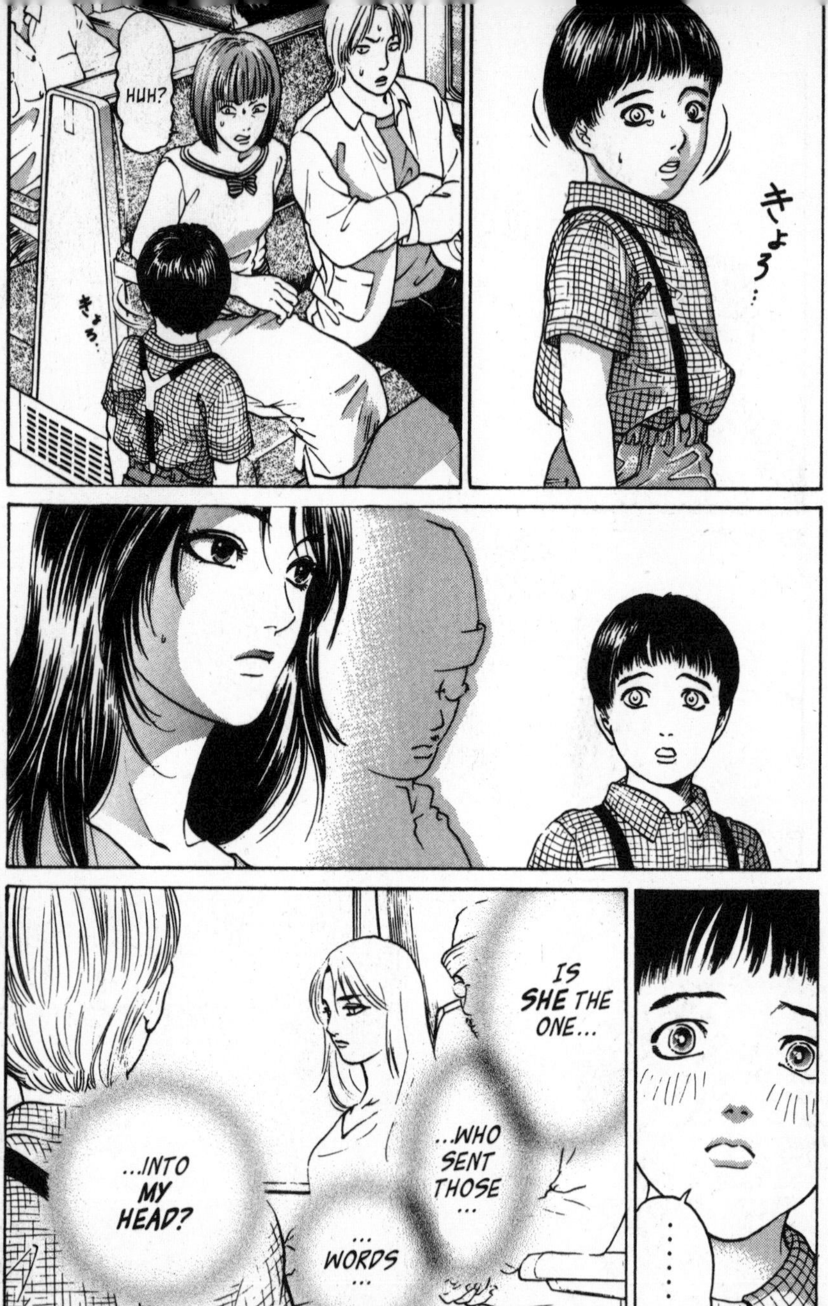

……

IS SHE THE ONE...

...WHO SENT THOSE...

...WORDS...

...INTO MY HEAD?

......
COME HERE.

HUH?

IF YOUR SON IS HUNGRY...
...I MIGHT HAVE SOMETHING FOR HIM TO EAT.
OH... O-OKAY.
HOW DARE SHE?!

I'VE GOT TO HELP HIM.

HE'S NEVER MET ANOTHER TELEPATH BEFORE.
THERE'S MUCH HE DOESN'T KNOW ABOUT OUR UNIQUE TALENTS.
LIGHT
Black Sesame Soft Cookies

COME OVER HERE.
O... OKAY...
I KNEW SHE WAS THE ONE...!
HOW OLD ARE YOU?
FOUR.
HOW DID SHE DO IT?
SHE'S SO COOL!

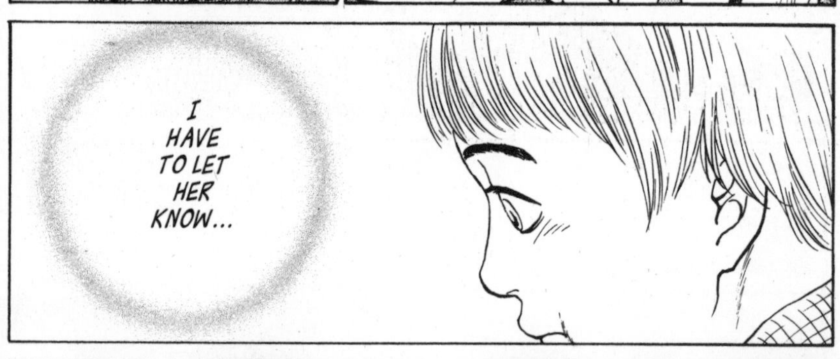

WHAT...?!

THIS MAN...
...HAS BEEN THINKING OF...
...BAD THINGS.
THIS OLD MAN...
...HE WANTS TO...
...TEAR OFF...
...HER CLOTHES.
UH...

I HAVE TO TELL HER.

BUT...

...THEN THE MAN...

...WILL GET ANGRY.

SO WILL MY MOM.

I WONDER...

...IF SHE CAN HEAR ME...

...IF I WARN HER IN MY **MIND?**

I HEAR YOU, NORIO!

I HEAR WHAT YOU'RE THINKING.

......

SO...

...YOU DON'T HAVE TO WORRY ABOUT IT ANYMORE.

BUT I DON'T--

SHH! DON'T ANSWER WITH YOUR VOICE!

YOU DON'T WHAT?
LISTEN ...

...JUST SAY, "NOTHING." UNDERSTAND?

N-NOTHING...

GOOD JOB!

HE'S PRETTY QUICK...
...FOR HIS AGE.
BUT EVEN STILL...
...HOW CAN A FOUR YEAR-OLD POSSIBLY UNDERSTAND THIS KIND OF POWER? I DON'T WANT HIM TO BE FRIGHTENED...

OH!!

MY HEAD ...!!
HE'S PROBING DEEP INTO MY MIND!

MIND READING
TELEPATH POWER
PSYCHIC POWER
TELEPATH
JUST YOU AND ME.
SPECIAL...
...EXISTENCE!
I THINK HE UNDERSTANDS!!
は..
......

DO OTHER PEOPLE KNOW WE CAN SEE WHAT'S INSIDE THEIR HEADS?!
OOPS.

THANK GOODNESS! THE NOISE OF THE TRAIN ENTERING THE TUNNEL...
...KEPT ANYONE ELSE FROM HEARING HIM!
ガタン
ガタン
ガタン
タン..
AH...
ドクンッ
ドクンッ
ドクーン
I TOLD YOU NOT TO SPEAK OUT LOUD!
ドクーン
OH!
I'M SORRY...!
I FOR-GOT...!
I'M REALLY, REALLY SORRY...

I WISH THAT KID WOULD GO BACK TO HIS SEAT.

PROBABLY NEVER GETS ATTENTION AT HOME.
BET THAT'S WHY HE'S SO EXCITED.
BUT IF HE DOESN'T MOVE SOON...
...I'LL KICK HIS LITTLE ASS!
......

NOT LONG AGO...

...MY MOTHER WAS THINKING OF PUSHING ME DOWN THE STAIRS.
SO I BEGGED HER...
...NOT TO DO IT.
SHE WAS VERY SURPRISED.

I SHOULDN'T HAVE ANSWERED...

...TO WHAT SHE WAS THINKING ABOUT.

......

THE TRAIN IS NEARLY OUT OF THE TUNNEL.

NORIO-KUN, WE HAVE TO STOP TALKING LIKE THIS.

WHAT?! WHY?!

HEY...

WERE YOU TWO SAYING BAD THINGS ABOUT ME?

HEY, I'M GOING TO THE RESTROOM.
HUH?!

THIS SO ISN'T GOOD...!

NORIO! KEEP QUIET!
N-NO!!

!
ER, C-CAN I GO WITH YOU?

NORIO! LEAVE THAT POOR GIRL ALONE!

......
OH, I DON'T MIND.

ガタン
タン・・
タタン・・
ジャー…

SO... DO YOU HAVE A FATHER?
YEAH... BUT...
...HE'S ALMOST NEVER HOME.
HE AND MOMMY FIGHT A LOT.
ジャー…

I DON'T THINK HE LIKES ME VERY MUCH.
HE'S NEVER HOME.
HE DRINKS A LOT, TOO.
SO... YOU STAY WITH YOUR MOM?
ガタン
タタン..

OH...! EXCUSE ME...!
.....?
....
!
IT'S OKAY.
THIS IS THE GIRL!!

ERR... MAY I...?

NO.
I-I MEAN...

WELL ...
IT'S JUST...

ふっ
STRANGE GUY...

YOU SEE...
HOW CAN I EXPLAIN THIS?

?
EXPLAIN WHAT?!
DAMN... I WASN'T EXPECTING HER TO BE SO BEAUTIFUL!
NOW I'M ALL TONGUE-TIED...
......
IT'S ABOUT...
ガタン
ゴトン
ザワ
...THE TRAIN...
ガターンッ

YOU...
...KNOW ABOUT THE CRASH?!
I KNEW IT!!
YOU PREDICTED THE LANDSLIDE TOO, DIDN'T YOU?!

THAT'S WHY YOU WILL MANAGE TO ESCAPE WITH ME.
PREDICTED?!
THAT EXPLAINS IT!
HOLD ME!
WHAT'S THE STRANGE MAN TALKING ABOUT?
GOOD... GOOD...

THE TRAIN ACCIDENT THAT THIS BOY AND I DREAMT ABOUT...
...WAS THE **FUTURE** THIS GUY **PREDICTED**!

WE SAW THE HORRIFIC IMAGES IN HIS MIND...

IS HE REALLY PSYCHIC?
WHEN...

...DID YOU PREDICT THE LAND-SLIDE?
ABOUT TWENTY MINUTES AGO.

TWENTY MINUTES AGO...
THAT'S ROUGHLY WHEN I WAS HAVING THE DREAM!

IS IT TRUE?!
IS IT?!
IS EVERYONE GOING TO DIE?!

YOU WON'T DIE.
HUH?!

HOW DOES HE KNOW...? CAN HE MAKE IT STOP?!

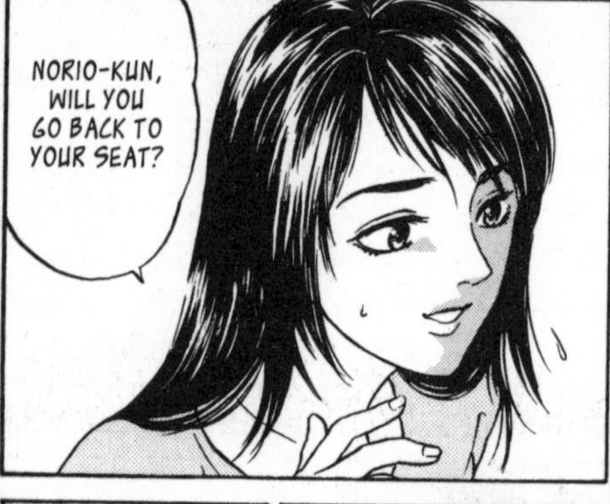
NORIO-KUN, WILL YOU GO BACK TO YOUR SEAT?

BUT...
I'LL FOLLOW YOU IN A MOMENT.
PLEASE.
OKAY...

......
YOUR LITTLE BROTHER?
UH... YEAH.
SOME-THING LIKE THAT...

!

......

WOW!

I WONDER IF SHE'D SLEEP WITH ME WHEN THIS IS OVER...?

WEREN'T YOU ABOUT TO SAY SOME-THING?

OH!

N-NO! I WASN'T...!

I BET SHE HAS SOME SEXY LINGERIE UNDER-NEATH HER CLOTHES.

MAYBE WE COULD RENT A ROOM NEARBY.

MAN-- I CAN'T WAIT TO FIND OUT!

SHE'S STILL ON HER GUARD...
I SHOULD TRY TO MAKE HER FEEL MORE COM-FORT-ABLE.
I'VE HAD THIS POWER SINCE I WAS A KID.
LUCKY
MADE IN U.S.A
FILTERS
I'VE NEVER BEEN WRONG. NOT ONCE.

YOU KNOW...
...IF YOU KEEP SMOKING THOSE THINGS...
...YOU'LL BECOME IMPOTENT.

OH, YEAH... I GUESS SO...
DAMN, I KEEP SCREWING UP!
NOTE TO SELF-- DON'T SMOKE AROUND HER!
HOW ABOUT YOU ...?

WHAT ABOUT ME?
YOUR ABILITY TO PREDICT THE FUTURE.
WELL, IT'S NOT AS GOOD AS YOURS...
BY THE WAY... WHERE'S YOUR SEAT?

タン
......
WHAT'S WRONG?
タタン
タン

WELL...

...WE BOTH KNOW THIS TRAIN...
...WILL DERAIL...
...RIGHT?
RIGHT!

DOESN'T HE CARE ABOUT THE OTHER PASSENGERS?

Episode 1: Two Psychics–Part 2 END

Episode 1: Two Psychics–Part 3

EVEN THOUGH WE KNOW WHAT'S GOING TO HAPPEN...

HUH?

...WE CAN'T HELP ANYONE... CAN WE?

I'M SUR-PRISED!
YOU, OF ALL PEOPLE, SHOULD KNOW THE ONE SIMPLE FACT ABOUT TRYING TO CHANGE THE FUTURE--
WHAT ?!
THAT IT'S IMPOS-SIBLE!
DON'T BE SO NAIVE!
HOW CAN YOU HAVE THIS POWER ...
...AND NOT UNDER-STAND THAT BY NOW ?!
SO...
...EVEN THOUGH ...
...WE HAVE SPECIAL POWERS...
...WE'RE NOT GOING TO DO ANY-THING?
HAVING A CON-SCIENCE IS...
...A WEAK-NESS!

THAT'S RIGHT.

IF YOU TELL ANYONE ABOUT YOUR PRE-DICTION...

...THEY'LL LAUGH.

NO ONE WILL BELIEVE YOU.

BUT ONCE YOUR PREDICTION COMES TRUE...

...EVERYONE WILL KNOW ABOUT YOUR POWER!

YOU'LL BE HUNTED...

...AND SCORNED!

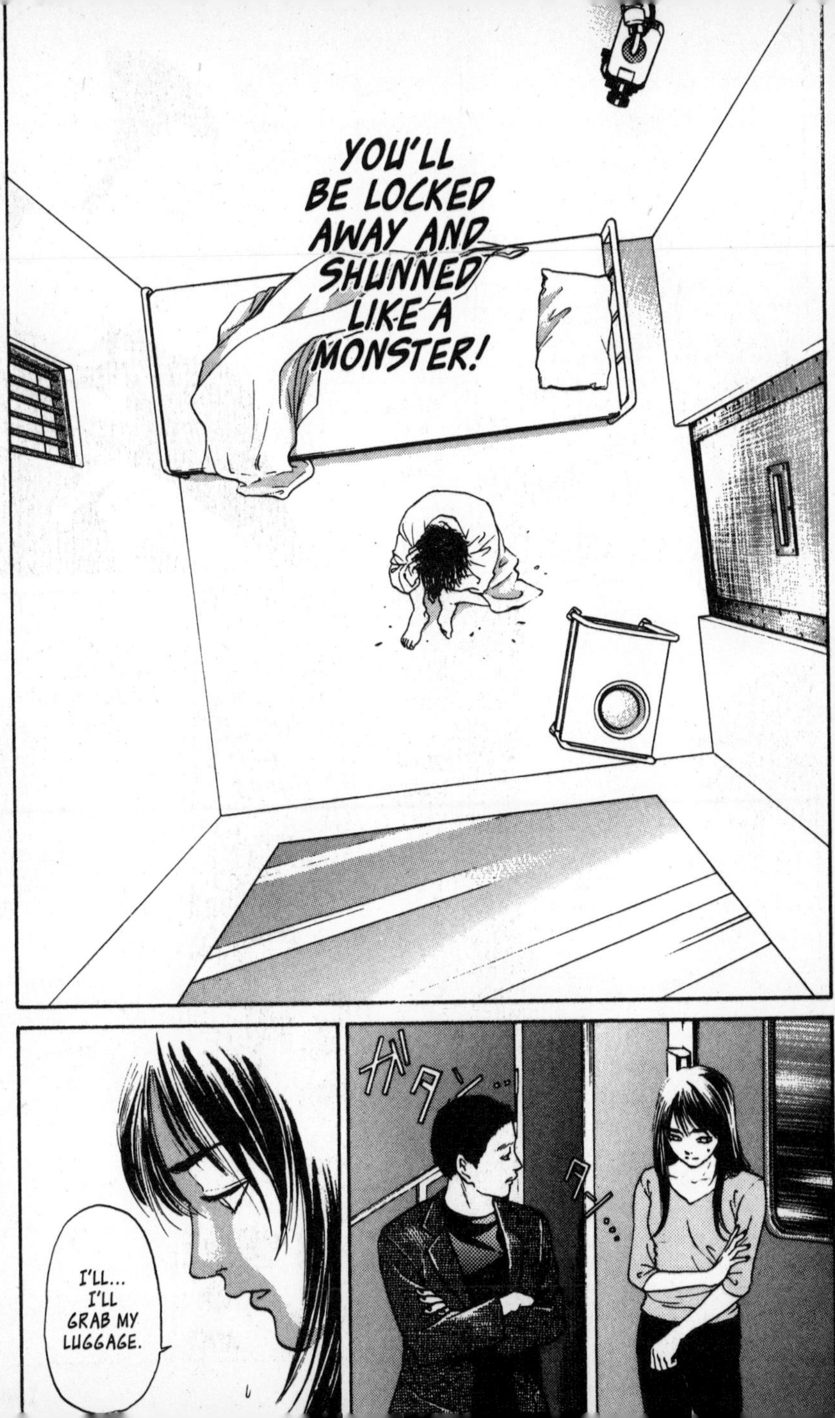

YOU'LL BE LOCKED AWAY AND SHUNNED LIKE A MONSTER!

ガ
カッ
"I CAN'T REMEMBER IF I TURNED OFF THE OVEN BEFORE I LEFT!"
"SHE THINKS I'M LYING..."
"I THINK HE'S LYING TO ME..."
"SHOULD I TELL HIM THIS IS OUR LAST TRIP TOGETHER?"
"WOW! IS SHE A MODEL?"
"LA LA LA... LA LA LA LA LA..."

"CRUMMY BOSS... MAKING ME WORK LATE..."
"WHY'S HE ACTING LIKE THIS?"
"I HOPE I GET HOME IN TIME TO WATCH THE GAME."
"IF THIS BUSINESS DEAL FALLS THROUGH, I'M GONNA KILL MY-SELF!"
"SO TIRED..."
"LA DEE DA, LA LA..."
HAVING A SOFT HEART NOW...
...IS A BIG MIS-TAKE.
A HEARTLESS MONSTER!
THAT'S WHAT I AM!

I'M GETTING OFF AT THE NEXT STATION...

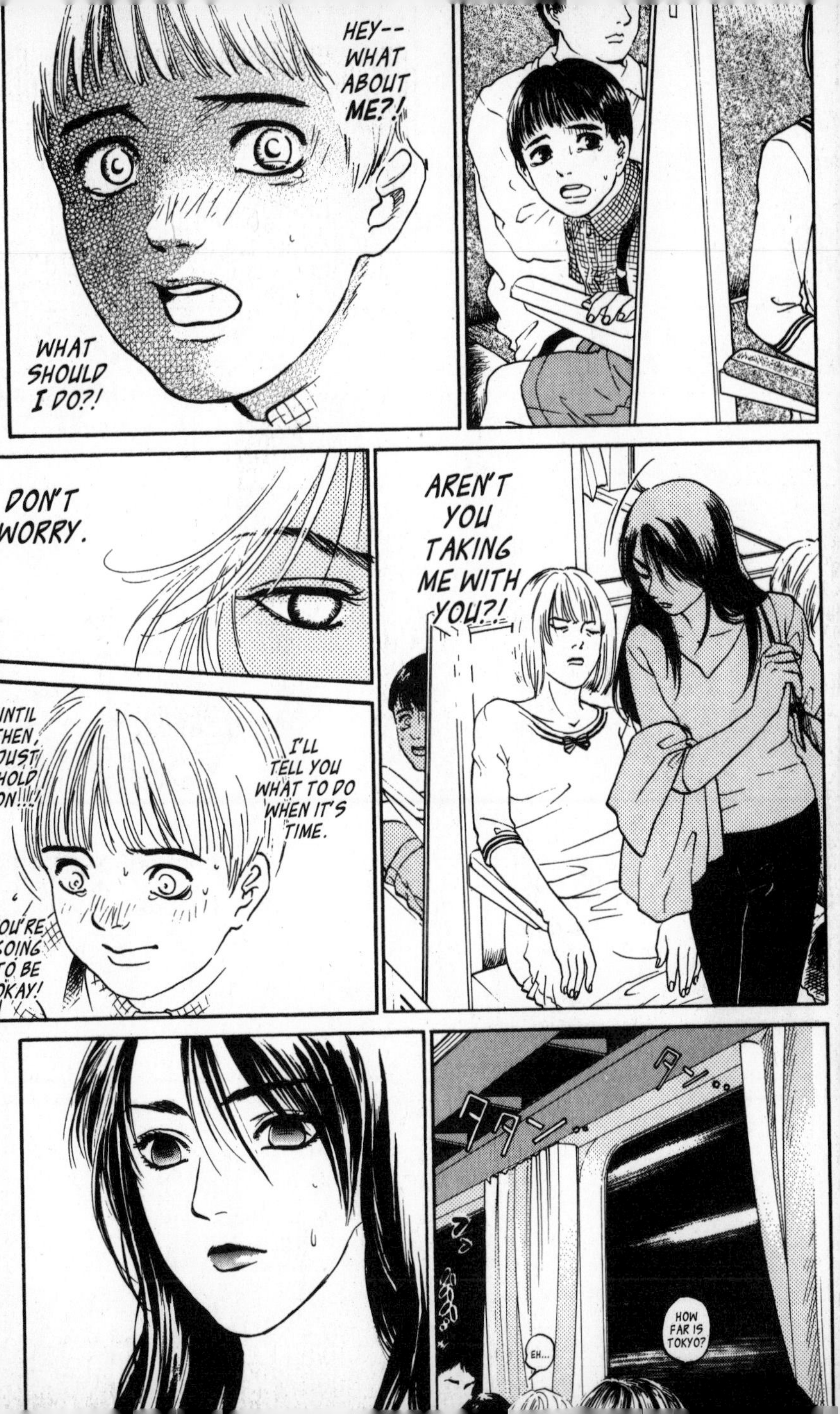

HEY-- WHAT ABOUT ME?!

WHAT SHOULD I DO?!

AREN'T YOU TAKING ME WITH YOU?!

DON'T WORRY.

I'LL TELL YOU WHAT TO DO WHEN IT'S TIME.

UNTIL THEN, JUST HOLD ON...!!

YOU'RE GOING TO BE OKAY!

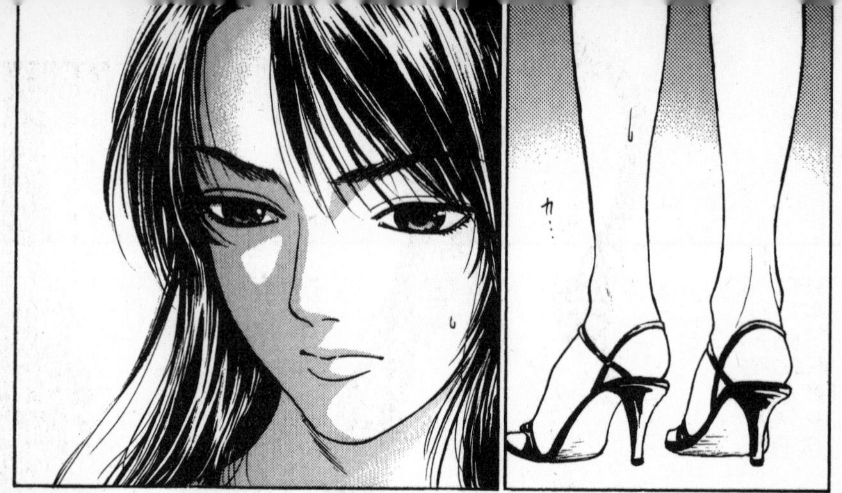
カ…

......
YOU KNOW...

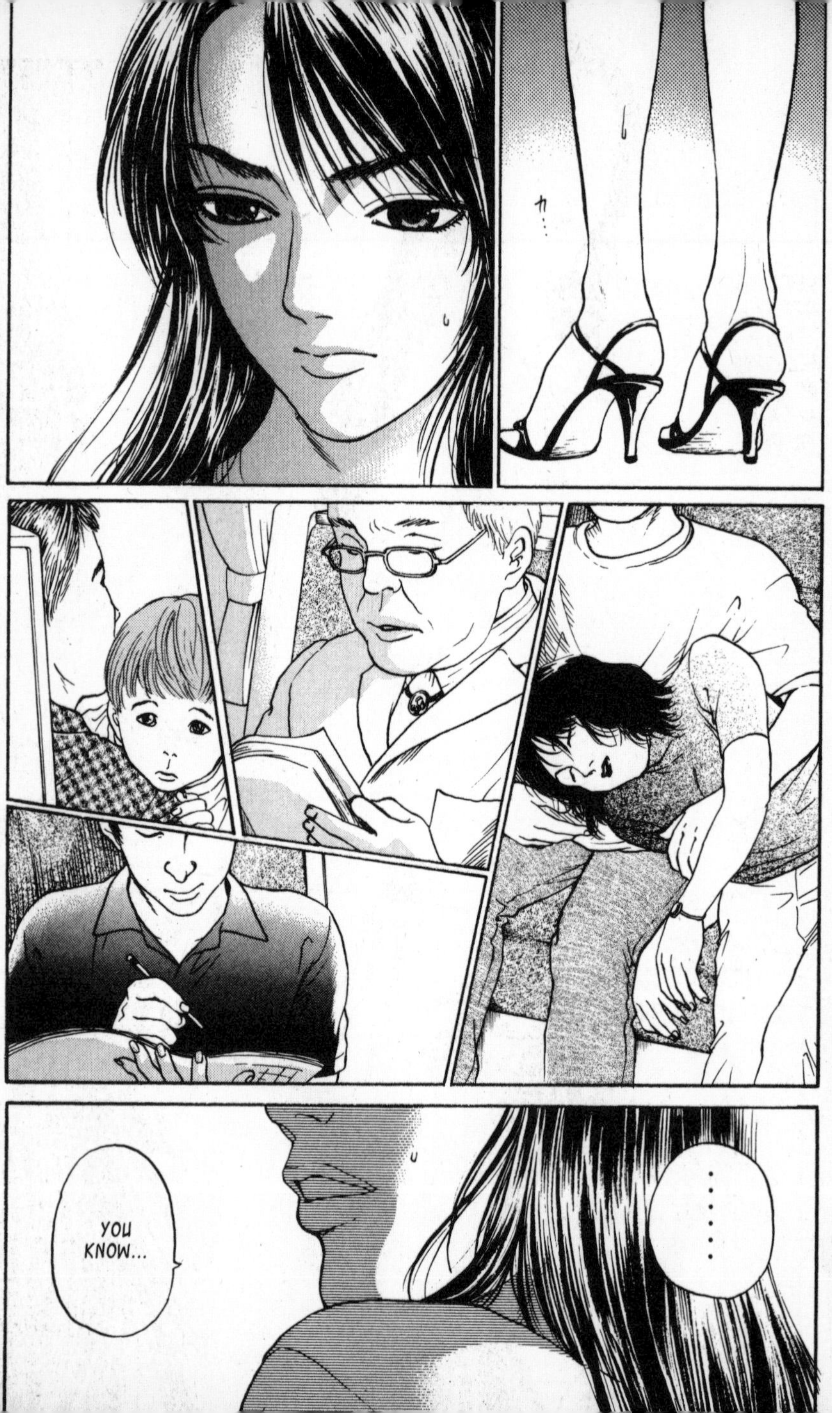

...I'M GETTING OFF THE TRAIN BECAUSE I'M AFRAID OF LAND-SLIDES.
SO... MAYBE *YOU* SHOULD *GET OFF* HERE, TOO.

WHAT'S SHE TALKING ABOUT...?
IDIOT!
SHUT UP!
HUH? IS SHE HAVING A FIGHT?
EMBAR-RASS-ING...
SORRY... BUT I REALLY HAVE TO GET TO TOKYO.
DUMB BITCH THINKS SHE KNOWS EVERY-THING....! IS SHE CRAZY OR WHAT?!
GO AWAY ALREADY, STUPID!
OH, JUST GO! PRETTY GIRLS MAKE ME SICK!
....

GOODBYE.

NEXT STOP-- SHIRAKABA STATION.
NORIO-KUN...
NORIO-KUN!
ANSWER ME!!

ガッ

OH… THERE SHE IS.

?

WAIT… WHAT'S SHE DOING?

はっ
HEY...!
O- OH...
WHY IS SHE ACTING SO WEIRD?
WHERE'S YOUR LITTLE BROTH- ER?
UH...
WHEN THE TRAIN STOPS...
...I'LL GET OFF ON THE OTHER SIDE...
...ALL BY MYSELF!
YEP!
I JUST GOTTA MAKE SURE...
...NO- BODY SEES ME...
WHAT?!

WAIT A SECOND...

*Note: Japanese usually do not add "kun" to a name when referring to a family me

HEY!!

HIS MOTHER...?
SHES'S ON BOARD, BUT...
LOOK-- I CAN'T LET HIM DIE!!
AW, SHIT...!
SHE'S NOT EVEN HIS REAL MOTHER!
PLUS, SHE'S ABUSING HIM!!
BESIDES ...

...I FINALLY FOUND SOMEONE ELSE LIKE ME...

......

I WON'T TELL YOU NOT TO TAKE HIM WITH YOU...

...BUT IF THAT BOY SURVIVES... AND HIS MOTHER DIES BECAUSE OF YOU...

...IT **WILL** MAKE THE **NEWS**.

……

……

LIAR!

EVEN I CAN'T PREDICT SO **PRECISELY**…

NO MATTER, THOUGH…

I'VE ALREADY SEEN THAT THE THREE OF US WALK OFF THIS TRAIN!

IT'S IMPOSSIBLE TO CHANGE THAT.

…

しらかば
白 樺
SHIRAKABA

ギギキィーッ

WELCOME TO SHIRAKABA STATION!

SO? WHERE IS HE?

HE SHOULD BE ON THE OTHER SIDE OF THE PLATFORM!

GOOD!
NORIO-KUN!!
IF YOU CAN HEAR ME--
--YOU MUST GO NOW!!
NORIO-KUN...?

?
......
HEY, LOOK! HE'S STILL UP THERE!
Yawn!

WHAT DO I DO?!
HELP ME!
HE'LL SEE ME!
I CAN'T GO!
DON'T LEAVE ME!
THIS IS BAD...
DON'T LET ME DIE!
BUT...MY PREDICTION CAN'T BE WRONG...
...CAN IT...?
I'LL NEVER...

...SEE HIM AGAIN!
NO...
RUN, NORIO!!
ビクッ
!
DUMB KID!

YOU... YOU CAME...
... BACK !!
NO TIME FOR HUGS! COME ON!!

SHE ...
SHE ...
SOME-BODY HELP !!

ドオーーッ
プシュー
ガタンッ
タン‥
タタン‥
タン‥

PANT...
PANT...
......
PANT...
WELL... I CERTAINLY DIDN'T PREDICT...
...THIS KIDNAP-PING!

ACT AS IF WE'RE A FAMILY.
HERE... TAKE MY HAND.

2
......
C'MON! WE GOTTA GO!
NOW... CASUALLY WALK TO THE OTHER SIDE OF THE PLATFORM.

......
I'M TAKING A TAXI TO A HOTEL IN SHIRA-KABAYAMA.
BUT YOU TWO...
...ARE GOING TO HOP ON A TRAIN THAT BYPASSES THE LANDSLIDE.
IS THIS REAL GOOD BYE?
SURE... THAT'S THE WAY I SAW IT. DIDN'T YOU?
I'LL SEE YOU OFF.
カン
カン
カン...
THANK YOU... FOR EVERY-THING.

MY VISION MAY HAVE SAVED US FOR NOW...
...BUT OUR PROBLEMS ARE FAR FROM OVER.
AFTER THE CCIDENT, OLICE ARE OING TO ARCH FOR US.
THIS CHICK DID SUCH A STUPID THING!
.....
DON'T CALL HER STUPID!

FOR YOUR SAFETY, PLEASE STAY BEHIND THE YELLOW LINE...

...

OOPS.

B-BUT ...!
THEY'RE TELEPATHS!!
TAKE CARE, TSUNEO!

Episode 1: Two Psychics Part 3 END

In Volume 2 of...

I...I can see your thoughts...
You really want me to read the author's mind and find out what's going to happen next. But Nanase says I'm not supposed to look... ow! All right! I'll do it! You don't have to think so loud, y'know...!

Okay...I see Nanase and me hiding in a big city with really tall buildings. Nanase, she's working at this loud place...with laughing... and alcohol. There are two men there...one is a nice man. But the other...he's a bad man. A real bad man that does bad things to girls...scary things...

Ooh! I see us on a really big boat and...who's that? The nice man is with us. I wonder why? Oh no! I read this one man's mind...and he's going to push his girlfriend overboard! We save her...but the police think we tried to hurt the girl?! But we didn't! We're the good guys! But help's on the way...from another psychic? Wait... There's another one like us on board?!
How many more like us are there?

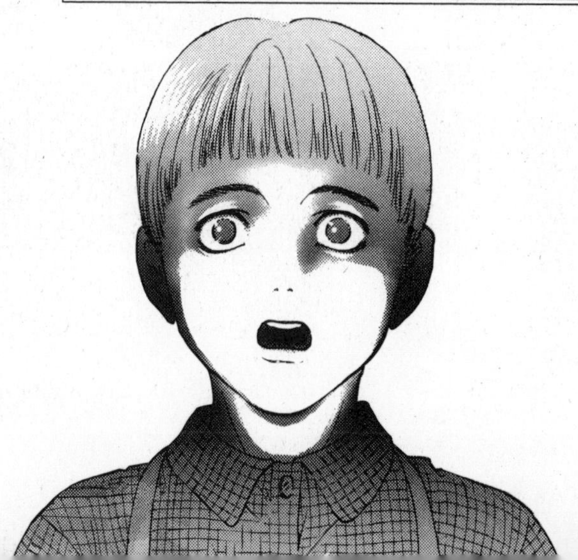

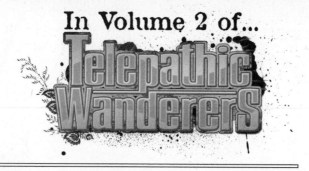

A MIDNIGHT OPERA™

Immortality, Redemption, and Bittersweet Love...

For nearly a millennium, undead creatures have blended into a Europe driven by religious dogma...

Ein DeLaLune is an underground Goth metal sensation on the Paris music scene, tragic and beautiful. He has the edge on other Goth music powerhouses—he's undead, a fact he's kept hidden for centuries. But his newfound fame might just bring out the very phantoms of his past from whom he has been hiding for centuries, including his powerful brother, Leroux. And if the two don't reconcile, the entire undead nation could rise up from the depths of modern society to lay waste to mankind.

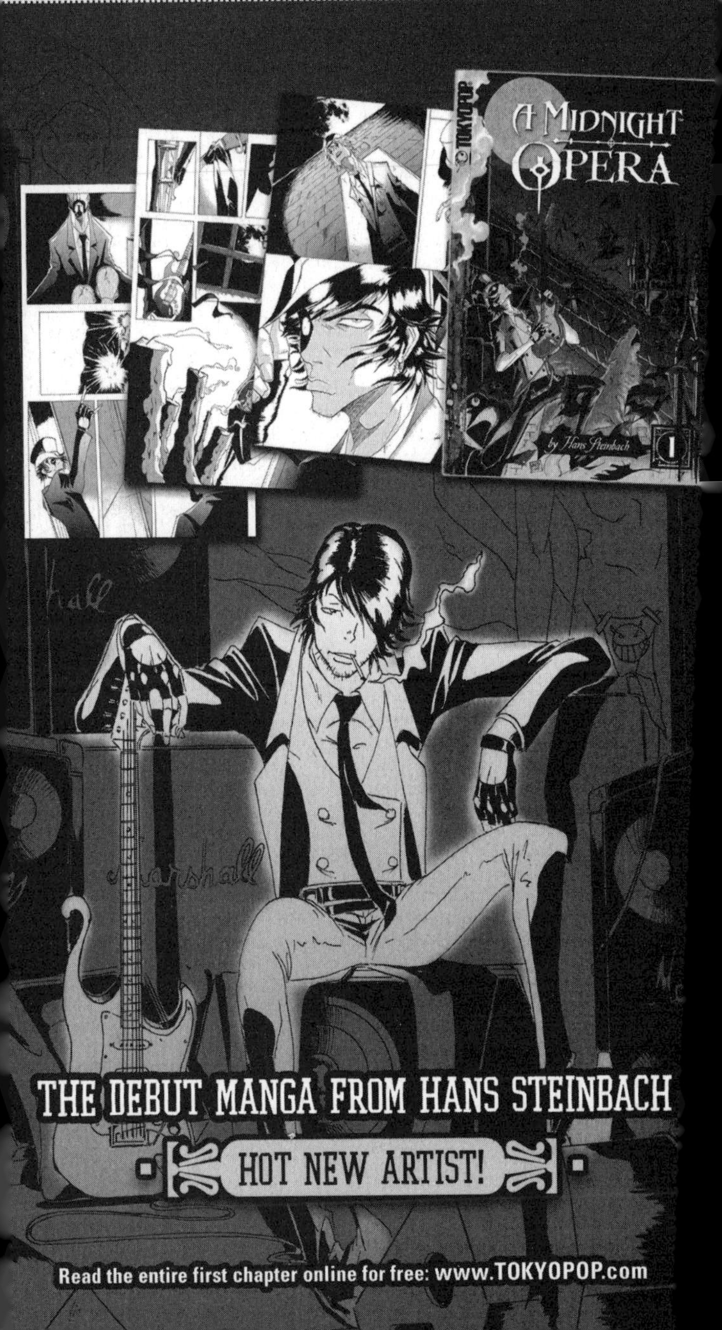

MARK OF THE SUCCUBUS

BY ASHLY RAITI & IRENE FLORES

Maeve, a succubus-in-training, is sent to the human world to learn how to hone her skills of seduction. But things get complicated when she sets her sights on Aiden, a smart but unmotivated student at her new high school. Meanwhile, the Demon World has sent a spy to make sure Maeve doesn't step out of line. And between Aiden's witchy girlfriend, his nutty best friend, and Demon World conspiracies, Maeve is going to be lucky to make it out of our world alive!

Here is a Gothic romantic fantasy set in one of the most menacing worlds known to humans: high school.

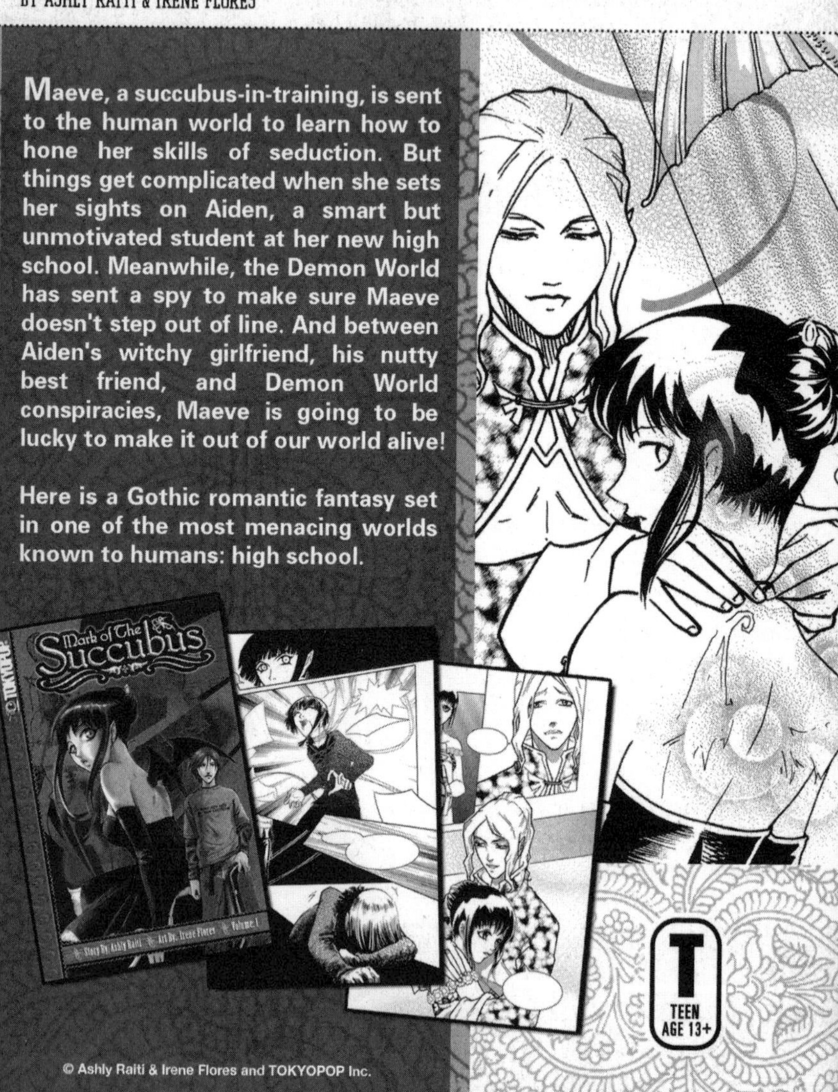

MANGA STUDIO™ 3.0

SPECIAL INTRODUCTORY PRICE FOR MANGA STUDIO 3.0 DEBUT:

$49.99

WHAT WILL *YOU* CREATE?

The Best Software For Digital Manga Creation

e frontier's Manga Studio lets you draw, ink, tone and letter your manga in the computer. A library of **1800 digital tones** uses vector technology for moiré-free results. Automated drawing tools speed the process of creating your sequential art. Twelve types of layers keep your work organized and easy to edit. Scan in existing artwork and finish it in the computer, saving time and money on materials. Manga Studio's 1200-dpi resolution ensures professional-quality files that can be saved in several popular formats.

For more information or to purchase, visit:
www.e-frontier.com/go/tokyopop

VAN VON HUNTER MANGA CREATED WITH MANGA STUDIO.

BY FUYUMI SORYO

MARS

I used to do the English adaptation for *MARS* and loved working on it. The art is just amazing—Fuyumi Soryo draws these stunning characters and beautiful backgrounds to boot. I remember this one spread in particular where Rei takes Kira on a ride on his motorcycle past this factory, and it's all lit up like Christmas and the most gorgeous thing you've ever seen—and it's a factory! And the story is a super-juicy soap opera that kept me on the edge of my seat just dying to get the next volume every time I'd finish one.

~Elizabeth Hurchalla, Sr. Editor

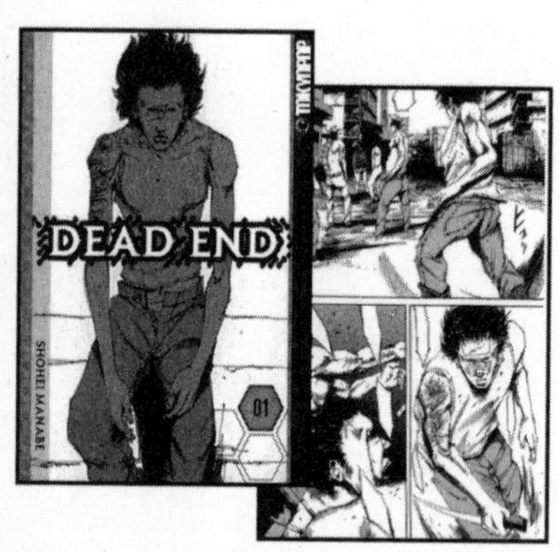

BY SHOHEI MANABE

DEAD END

Everyone I've met who has read *Dead End* admits to becoming immediately immersed and obsessed with Shohei Manabe's unforgettable manga. If David Lynch, Clive Barker and David Cronenberg had a love child that was forced to create a manga in the bowels of a torture chamber, then *Dead End* would be the fruit of its labor. The unpredictable story follows a grungy young man as he pieces together shattered fragments of his past. Think you know where it's going? Well, think again!

~Troy Lewter, Editor

STEADY BEAT

BY RIVKAH

"Love Jessica"... That's what Leah finds on the back of a love letter to her sister. But who is Jessica? When more letters arrive, along with flowers and other gifts, Leah goes undercover to find out her sister's secret. But what she doesn't expect is to discover a love of her own—and in a very surprising place!

Winner of the Manga Academy's Create Your Own Manga competition!

T TEEN AGE 13+

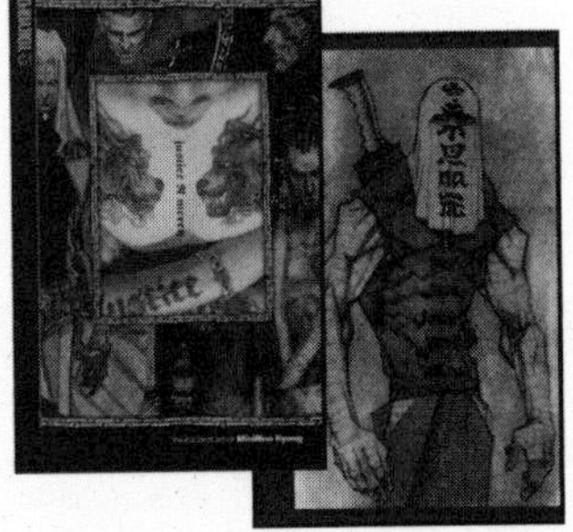

JUSTICE N MERCY

BY MIN-WOO HYUNG

Min-Woo Hyung is one of today's most talented young Korean artists, and this stunning art book shows us why. With special printing techniques and high-quality paper, TOKYOPOP presents never-before-seen artwork based on his popular *Priest* series, as well as images from past and upcoming projects *Doomslave, Hitman* and *Sal.*

A spectacular art book from the creator of *Priest!*

T TEEN AGE 13+

MOBILE SUIT GUNDAM SEED NOVEL

ORIGINAL STORY BY HAJIME YATATE AND YOSHIYUKI TOMINO

WRITTEN BY LIU GOTO

A shy young student named Kira Yamato is thrown in the midst of battle when genetically enhanced Coordinators steal five new Earth Force secret weapons. Wanting only to protect his Natural friends, Kira embraces his Coordinator abilities and pilots the mobile suit Strike. The hopes and fears of a new generation clash with the greatest weapons developed by mankind: Gundam!

The novelization of the super-popular television series!

T TEEN AGE 13+

STOP!

This is the back of the book. You wouldn't want to spoil a great ending!

This book is printed "manga-style," in the authentic Japanese right-to-left format. Since none of the artwork has been flipped or altered, readers get to experience the story just as the creator intended. You've been asking for it, so TOKYOPOP® delivered: authentic, hot-off-the-press, and far more fun!

DIRECTIONS

If this is your first time reading manga-style, here's a quick guide to help you understand how it works.

It's easy... just start in the top right panel and follow the numbers. Have fun, and look for more 100% authentic manga from TOKYOPOP®!